Business in Korea
A guide for foreigners

2nd Edition

Includes Explanations of Cultural Nuances

New Sections on Startups and Getting a Job in Korea

Now Includes Korean Phrasebook

Robert Oakley

No part of this publication may be replicated, redistributed, or given away in any form without the written consent of the author.

Contents

Introduction	4
Note to the reader	7
South Korea	8
Korean Language and Useful Phrases	9
Numbers	17
Respect, Age, and status	23
Positions and Titles	25
Working Hours	27
Hweshik (Staff Meal)	29
Gender Equality	31
Korean names	32
Introductions	33
Meetings	34
Business cards	38
Gift giving	39
The importance of colour	39
Building relationships	40
Dinner Invitations	41
The Dark Side of Business	42
Home Invitations	43
Dining Etiquette	44
Uniquely Korean traits	46
Maintaining face	47
Gibun (기분)	47
Nunchi (눈치)	47

Business in Korea A guide for foreigners 2nd Edition

Jeong (정)	**48**
Han (한)	**48**
Getting a Job in Korea	**49**
The Korean Startup Ecosystem	**56**
Registering a Business in Korea	**65**
Marketing in Korea	**67**
Index	**69**

Introduction

Thank you for choosing
Business Korean *A guide for foreigners* 2nd Edition.

Who is this book for?

This book is for people who do business in Korea or do business with Koreans. Maybe you work in a Korean company, travel to Korea for business, maybe you are a student, or maybe you are a founder looking for a base to launch your startup, whatever your reason... if you want to learn the art of business in Korea, and gain an understanding of business culture and etiquette to help you succeed in business with Koreans, then this book is for you.

So why the 2nd Edition? Korea is such a fast-moving country that a lot has changed in the two years since I wrote this book. I also wanted to add sections about startups, how to get a Job in Korea, and a section about the Korean language (Including a phrase book)

Why did I write this book?

The idea for this book came to me while I was living and working in South Korea. I was working for a Korean IT company, not a Korean branch of an international company, but a Korean Company. And for the majority of my time there, I was the only foreigner among a staff of 1,000+ employees. I had a basic grasp of Korean but desperately needed to learn the cultural nuances relevant to business.

I wanted to update and expand my work on the first edition of this book, as there were a number of additional sections I wanted to include; such as a section on the Korean language, a section on getting a Job in Korea, and also for it to have more of a focus on the massive opportunity for startups that this fascinating nation presents.

Korea is continuing to grow in power and influence and many countries now enjoy free trade with Korea and closer business ties. Even during and following the global pandemic, Korea has still been investing in a world-leading global startup ecosystem and their agile response to the covid-19 undoubtedly saved many lives by containing the virus and reducing its spread, whilst also avoiding any lockdowns.

This book is to help *you* do business with Korea.

About me

I have over 25 years of experience in Business, in Europe, Australia and Korea.

I have taught Business English for a number of years and consulted and coached students on the differences between Korean and Western approaches to business. For over seven years, I worked in South Korea in Global Enterprise software, High tech, and startup sectors, as a Marketing Professional. In 2020 I returned to the UK with my family and have, of course, maintained a keen interest in Korean language culture and business.

Note to the reader

While every effort has been made to make this guide as useful as possible in preparing you for doing business in Korea, I must point out an obvious fact. Human beings are individuals and behaviours and expectations vary as much within a country as they do between east and west. Please use your own discretion and intelligence when conducting business with Koreans, not all Koreans are the same. Use this book as a guide and it should put you on the right foot to succeed in Business in Korea.

South Korea

South Korea: 한국 (Hanguk) or officially the Republic of Korea: 대한민국 (Daehan Minguk), is located on the Korean Peninsula of the Asian continent and is 100,188.1 km^2 in size. This is 45% of the total area of 221,000 km^2 which includes the whole Korean Peninsula both South and North and its annexed islands. Korea's best-known islands include Jeju Island, Geoje Island, Jin Island and Ulleung Island.

Three sides of the peninsula are coastal, with the Yellow Sea in the west, the East Sea in the east and the South Sea in the south. The remaining side is separated from North Korea along the 38th parallel by the DMZ (Demilitarized Zone).

TIP: When in Korea avoid displaying maps or referring to the *East Sea* as the *Sea of Japan*. This is a contentious issue in the region and at least will create awkwardness, at worst cause offence.

Korean Language and Useful Phrases

Korean may look difficult to read at first glance, but it is actually possible to learn the Korean Alphabet in just a few hours. But then comes blending consonants and diphthongs - and things start to get complicated. And when you get into grammar and sentence structure, things really get complicated! However - Koreans will be really impressed if you can say a few polite words in Korean and make an effort, and in business that can really go a long way in showing respect and that you are serious about building relationships.

TIP: Korean is easy to learn but really difficult to master! However, any effort you make to learn Korean will go a long way to forging strong business relationships

---

Vowels

Korean vowels can be short or long, but this is not shown in written Korean

a ㅏ   like 'a' in "f**a**ther"

o ㅗ   like 'o' in "t**o**ne"

eo (ŏ) ㅓ   like the "uh" in "l**u**st"

u ㅜ   A low sound of "oo" as in "h**oo**p". "w**oo**"

eu (ŭ) ㅡ   like 'i' in "cous**i**n", "d**o**zen".

i ㅣ   like the 'i' in "sh**i**p" (short) OR the 'ee' in "sh**ee**p" (long)

e ㅔ   like the 'e' in "b**e**d"

ae ㅐ   similar to the "a" in "c**a**ve", "sp**a**ce", "b**ai**t", and "p**ay**"

Consonants

Most Korean consonants can be pronounced in three ways; **aspirated, unaspirated** and **tensed** (stressed).

b (p) ㅂ   like 'p' in "s**p**it" (unaspirated)

p (p', ph) ㅍ   like 'p' in "**p**ig" (aspirated)

pp ㅃ   tensed 'p', like 'p' in "**p**etit" in French

d (t) ㄷ   like 't' in "s**t**ab" (unaspirated)

t (t', th) ㅌ   like 't' in "**t**op" (aspirated)

tt ㄸ		tensed 't'
g (k) ㄱ		like 'k' in "skate" (unaspirated)
k (k', k) ㅋ		like 'c' in "cat" (aspirated)
kk ㄲ		tensed 'k'
j (ch) ㅈ		like 'g' in "gin" (unaspirated)
ch (ch') ㅊ		like 'ch' in "chin" (aspirated).
jj ㅉ		tensed 'j'
s ㅅ		like 's' in "soon", 'sh' before *i* or any "y" dipthong.
ss ㅆ		tensed 's', 's' in 'sea', never 'sh'
n ㄴ		like 'n' in "nice"
m ㅁ		like 'm' in "mother"
l ㄹ		between 'l', 'r' and 'n',
h ㅎ		like 'h' in "help"

ng ㅇ   like 'ng' in "sing". Unpronounced when at the start of a syllable.

The above pronunciations are correct for the first consonant, but the consonants in the middle of a word are usually **voiced**.

Diphthongs

Korean has two standalone diphthongs:

oe ㅚ   like 'we' in 'west'

ui ㅢ   like 'ŭ' + 'i'

Most vowels can be modified by prefixing them with 'y' or 'w':

wa ㅘ   like 'wa' sound in "s**ua**ve"

wae ㅙ like 'wa' in "**wa**ve".

wo ㅝ like 'wuh' sound in "**wo**nder"

wi ㅟ like "**we**" or 'e' in "sh**e**" with rounded lips

we ㅞ like 'we' in "**we**st"

ya ㅑ like 'ya' in "**ya**rd"

yo ㅛ like 'yo' in "**Yo**rk".

yeo (yŏ) ㅕ like 'you' in "**you**ng"

yu ㅠ   like "**you**"

ye ㅖ   like 'ye' in "**ye**s"

yae ㅒ   like 'ye' in "**ye**s"

Greetings and Goodbyes

Hello. (*most formal*)
  안녕 하십니까. (*annyeong hasimnikka*). Reply in the same way

Hello. (*formal*)
  안녕하세요. (*annyeonghaseyo*) to older people or to the people you meet first time

Hello. (*informal*)
  안녕. (*annyeong*) to your friends or younger people. Children will say this.

Hello. (*on the phone*)
  여보세요. (*yeoboseyo*) when you answer the phone.

Goodbye. (*to person leaving*)
  안녕히 가세요. (*annyeonghi gaseyo*)

Goodbye (*to person staying*)
  안녕히 계세요. (*annyeonghi gyeseyo*)

Goodbye (*informal*)
  안녕. (*annyeong*)

TIP: When you greet people say *annyeong hasimnikka* and bow, or offer your right hand with the left hand under your right elbow and give a firm handshake.

Introductions

What is your name?
성함(이름)이 어떻게 되세요? (*seonghami eotteoke doeseyo?*)

My name is _____ .
제 이름은 __ __입니다. (*je ireumeun ____-imnida*)

I am _____. (*my name is*)
저는 _____입니다 (*jeoneun _____-imnida*)

Nice to meet you.
만나서 반갑습니다. (*mannaseo ban-gapseumnida*)

How are you?
어떻게 지내세요? (*eotteoke jinaeseyo?*)

Fine, thank you.
잘 지냅니다, 감사합니다. (*jal jinaemnida, gamsahamnida*)

TIP: Koreans like to find out personal details that they feel are important, such as your age, your nationality/ethnicity, what university you graduated from, and even your salary. These are all important to establish social status, so try not to be offended.

Polite words

Please.
    부탁합니다. (*butakamnida*)

Thank you.
    감사합니다. (*gamsahamnida*)

You're welcome.
    천만에요. (*cheonmanyeyo*)

Yes.
    예/네. (*ye/ne*)

No.
    아니요. (*aniyo*)

Excuse me. (*getting attention*)
    실례합니다. (*sillyehamnida*)

I'm sorry.
    죄송합니다. (*joesonghamnida*)

Learning More

How do you say _____ in Korean?

_____은 한국말로 어떻게 말합니까?

_____-eun hangungmallo eotteoke malhamnikka?

What is this/that called?

이것은/저것은 무엇이라고 부릅니까?

igeoseun/jeogeoseun mu-eosirago bureumnikka?

Days

Today	오늘 (*oneul*)	This week	이번 주 (*ibeon ju*)
Yesterday	어제 (*eoje*)	Last week	지난 주 (*jinan ju*)
Tomorrow	내일 (*naeil*)	Next week	다음 주 (*da-eum ju*)

Days of the week

Sunday	일요일 (*iryoil*)	Thursday	목요일 (*mogyoil*)
Monday	월요일 (*woryoil*)	Friday	금요일 (*geumyoil*)
Tuesday	화요일 (*hwayoil*)	Saturday	토요일 (*toyoil*)
Wednesday	수요일 (*suyoil*)		

Numbers

In a business meeting, it is inevitable that Numbers will be discussed. There are distinct differences between the number systems used for counting in Korea and the West, which can cause confusion.

Large numbers are confusing as Koreans and other countries in Northeast Asia count in groups of four digits (10,000, 100,000,000) rather than in thousands.

This can make converting large numbers between English and Korean quite a challenge.

To Koreans, 5 million is 500 ten thousands.

For clarity, it is advisable to write out the entire number with all its digits.

TIP: When discussing large numbers, write out the whole number with all the digits, and give Koreans time to understand the number before continuing.

Counting

Koreans view counting as a reference to the units of time that a condition existed. So Koreans start counting at one. You are one year old when you are born. An overnight trip is a two-day trip etc.

Sino-Korean numbers

Sino-Korean numbers are used for amounts of currency, telephone numbers, the 24-hour clock and counting minutes.

0	공 (gong) / 영 (yeong)	10	십 (sip)
1	일 (il)	11	십일 (sibil)
2	이 (i)	12	십이 (sibi)
3	삼 (sam)	13	십삼 (sipsam)
4	사 (sa)	14	십사 (sipsa)
5	오 (o)	15	십오 (sibo)
6	육 (yuk)	16	십육 (simnyuk)
7	칠 (chil)	17	십칠 (sipchil)
8	팔 (pal)	18	십팔 (sip-pal)
9	구 (gu)	19	십구 (sipgu)

20	이십 (isip)	100,000	십만 (simman)
21	이십일 (isibil)	1,000,000	백만 (baengman)
22	이십이 (isibi)	10,000,000	천만 (cheonman)
23	이십삼 (isipsam)	100,000,000	억 (eok)
30	삼십 (samsip)	1,000,000,000	십억 (sibeok)
40	사십 (sasip)	10,000,000,000	백억 (baegeok)
50	오십 (osip)		
60	육십 (yuksip)	100,000,000,000	천억 (cheoneok)
70	칠십 (chilsip)	1,000,000,000,000 (one trillion)	조 (jo)
80	팔십 (palsip)		
90	구십 (gusip)	10,000,000,000,000	십조 (sipjo)
100	백 (baek)		
200	이백 (ibaek)	100,000,000,000,000	백조 (baekjo)
300	삼백 (sambaek)	1,000,000,000,000,000	천조 (cheonjo)
1,000	천 (cheon)		
2,000	이천 (icheon)	10,000,000,000,000,000	경 (gyeong)
10,000	만 (man)		

Native Korean Numbers

Numbers above 100 are always counted with Sino-Korean numbers.

1	하나 (hana)		11	열하나 (yeolhana)
2	둘 (dul)		20	스물 (seumul)
3	셋 (set)		30	서른 (seoreun)
4	넷 (net)		40	마흔 (maheun)
5	다섯 (daseot)		50	쉰 (swin)
6	여섯 (yeoseot)		60	예순 (yesun)
7	일곱 (ilgop)		70	일흔 (ilheun)
8	여덟 (yeodeol)		80	여든 (yeodeun)
9	아홉 (ahop)		90	아흔 (aheun)
10	열 (yeol)			

Counting words

When counting objects in Korean we use special counting words. For example, "two bottles" is *dubyeong* (2병), where *du* is "two" and *-byeong* means "bottles".

Objects 개 *-gae*

People 명 *-myeong*, 분 *-bun* (polite)

flat paper-like objects (papers, tickets, pages) 장 *-jang*

Bottles 병 *-byeong*

Cups, glasses 잔 *-jan*

Animals 마리 *-mari*

Times 번 *-beon*

Machines 대 *-dae*

Long objects (pens) 자루 *-jaru*

Small boxes 갑 *-gap*

Books 권 *-gwon*

Large boxes 상자 *-sangja*

Letters, phone calls, e-mails 통 *-tong*

Boats 척 *-cheok*

Bunches e.g. flowers 송이 *-song-i*

TIP: For numbers 1 through 4 as well as 20 when combined with a counting word, the last letter of the number is dropped: one person is *hanmyeong* (*hana+myeong*), two tickets is *dujang* (*dul+jang*), three things is *segae* (*set+gae*), four things is *negae* (*net+gae*), twenty things is *seumugae* (*seumul+gae*).

Respect, Age, and status

The following is an important section that should help you understand one of the most significant aspects of Korean culture, stemming from its Confucian roots.

Koreans hold a deep respect for those with more advanced age and higher status. This is one of the most important observations one will make while observing how Koreans conduct themselves in meetings and in the workplace in general.

Getting a good understanding of this can help you greatly in navigating the business landscape. It is SO important in Korean culture, that hierarchy affects all aspects of social interactions. A side effect of this is that everyone has a role in society as a result of hierarchy - therefore it is vital to respect it.

Koreans are most comfortable interacting with someone they consider their equal. In its most basic form, age is the base criteria. Simply, unless you are the same age you won't be classed as a friend.

This is ingrained in Korean culture from an early age, for example when my family arrived in Korea in 2012 my son was 5 years old and went to the play area, there were some older boys playing there and they played together for some time.

My son proudly said that they were his first friends in Korea and was mortified when they replied - "oh we are not friends, you are only 5, we are 6 years old".

In case you are wondering, yes he did get over it and went on to make lots of 'true' friends in Korea.

Status can be determined by someone's role in an organisation, the organisation they work for, the university they went to and their marital status.

In Business, you will notice that Koreans let those with seniority lead the proceedings, speak first, and make decisions. While assuming a lower position for themselves.

TIP: Be polite and respectful at all times, it may sound obvious but be careful, what is acceptable in the west may be frowned upon in Korea.

Positions and Titles

Korea has several systems for defining positions in a company. I have included the most common system here. Where there are two equivalent positions in English below one may be omitted in the Korean company or one may be used to denote a slightly higher grade or longer service.

Let's start with Junior positions in office Jobs

한글	Romanization	English
신입사원	Shinip Sawon	Graduate / new employee
사원	Sawon	Regular Staff / Assistant
주임	Joolm	Assistant Manager
대리	DaeRi	Assistant Manager
과장	KwaJang	Manager
차장	ChaJag	Senior Manager
부장	BooJang	Head Manager
팀장	Team Jang	Team Leader
실장	ShilJang	Department Head

Now, let's look at the Senior (Executive) positions

이사	EeSsa	Director
상무	SangMoo	Vice President
전무	JeonMoo	Executive Vice President
사장	SaJang	President
회장	HuiJang	Chairman

TIP: You can address business acquaintances simply by their title + nim e.g. Daeri Nim, or by their family name + title + nim e.g. Kim Daeri Nim

Working Hours

Working hours in Korea are among some of the highest in the OECD.

Until a few years ago it was common to work a 6-day week, or at least a 5.5-day week.

The rules

Officially you will see 2 numbers promoted. "Working hours shall not exceed forty hours a week and eight hours a day, excluding recess hours". And a government-mandated Maximum 52 Hour week. But not all companies fall under these restrictions. Smaller companies, for example, are exempt.

The reality

The reality is quite different. When the 52 Hour week rule was introduced in 2018, I was working for an enterprise software company. Nothing much changed in the working culture, and there were even rumours of underhand practices on the timekeeping system (default to 9am regardless of when you clock in) to help keep official reporting on target.

However, most office workers do not start their working day much before 8:30am, but when the day ends is often a complicated beast.

Again, not so common today, although I know first-hand this still takes place is the 'obligation to stay' until the boss goes home. This is often abused by the boss, who intentionally delays his leaving time either as a punishment or due to his own sadistic will. A particularly cruel boss may have the habit of arranging meetings as late as 9 pm in the evening, that drag on for hours. Before announcing that he wants to drink and that the 'team' should accompany him.

Night work

There is also the all too common '야간' ya'gan which translates as night work. This occurs frequently due to urgent work, last minute prep for meetings with the CEO the next day and sometimes 'sadistic will'.

야간 is never paid overtime and you will often see exhausted workers, catching the last subway, or night bus, amongst the equally exhausted and drunken participants of a hwe'shik (see next chapter).

Hweshik (Staff Meal)

A Hweshik '회식' is dinner with co-workers but depending on the occasion has a very specific and important purpose.

Koreans love to shorten and fuse words to come up with new words that have a specific meaning, and once you start to understand the language you can really appreciate these fused words.

"Hwe" means a gathering and "Shik" comes from the word "Shik-sa".

You may have a Hweshik when new employees join a company. Before this very important occasion, it will be difficult to feel part of the team, make friends or even be trusted, amongst your new colleagues. There will also be a Hweshik when someone leaves the company.

Most companies will also have a Hweshik regularly, for example monthly, or for a team member's birthday.

Other occasions will be the end of the year or the end of a project, a retirement.

There may be specific nuances depending on the company, but the food will be great.

Every attendee will be expected to join in multiple group-wide toasts. And mingle with other colleagues often by taking a clean glass and bottle of Soju around the table for a shot, the glass is usually shared and you take turns politely pouring a glass for each other and downing your shot.

These are official gatherings and their purpose is very different from a casual chicken and beer after work.

In some cases, a small amount is deducted from salaries to contribute to these regular gatherings.

If you are working at a Korean company either on a project or as a permanent or temporary employee you will most likely be 'invited' to a hweshik. These are compulsory events and refusal will likely cause offence. Consider it an honour rather than an obligation to attend such an event

---

TIP: Try to get involved as much as you can, there are numerous toasts, cheers, and speeches. Your colleagues will genuinely want to see what kind of person you are so try to be open and sociable.

Gender Equality

Korea, at times, seems years behind the west when it comes to gender equality. Things are improving, but it is still rare that Korean women will hold senior positions in a company.

One trend I have noticed is that a growing number of young Korean women are launching their own businesses, especially in the cosmetic and fitness industries and these are often startups.

However Korean women are expected to leave the workforce soon after marriage and start a family, with very few returning to work as the children grow up.

Unfortunately, due to the high levels of unemployment among young people, it is almost impossible for women over 40 to find office-based roles, without significant prior experience or connections.

Korean names

Korean family names are composed of one syllable, while given names tend to have two. You may come across Koreans who have a one-syllable first name, but this is less common.

The family name is put first, followed by the first name (as in Kim Jong-min). Koreans do not have middle names.

The family names, Kim 김, Park 박, and Lee 이, are most common

In formal business settings, you should use the formal title and surname (As in Chairman Park). Or Use the family name preceded by Mr or Mrs.

Follow this rule whether speaking directly to someone or about them to another Korean person. Yes, you should be polite when talking to or even referring to another person.

These days many Koreans, especially in business, use Western first names and prefer that it is used instead of their family name.

TIP: Address your Hosts as "Mr" + FamilyName, or FamilyName + "Nim" 님 or in a business setting "Title" + Family Name (e.g. Chairman Park) until told another way to address them.

Introductions

Introductions are usually made by a third person, therefore it is best to wait to be introduced to a business contact.

Similarly, when first establishing contact, it's best to use an intermediary party known to both of you, as cold calls are rarely responded to in South Korea.

Koreans value relationship ties and the strongest of these are blood ties, school or university ties, and work ties.

Even if two parties have never met, the fact that they attended the same school or university, even at completely different times, will be a welcome and firm basis on which to build any future business relationship.

TIP: Trade Shows are a good way to facilitate an introduction without an intermediary. In my experience, it is acceptable to follow up with the company after meeting a company representative at a trade show.

Meetings

In South Korea, business meetings usually take place in mid-morning (10 am -12 pm) or mid-afternoon (2-4 pm).

Use these times as a guide when suggesting a meeting.

When scheduling a meeting, plan well ahead of time.

South Koreans appreciate punctuality. So, try not to arrive more than a few minutes early and, of course, try not to be late.

Arriving too early or too late disrupts their schedule and, especially being late, may be interpreted as a sign of disrespect on your part. If you know you are going to be late, let them know as soon as possible and make sure you apologize, even if it is not your fault.

If your Korean counterparts cancel the meeting on a number of occasions it might mean that they're not really committed to working with you, or that there is a major issue that needs to be addressed before your negotiations can continue.

Be sensitive to repeated cancellations.

TIP: Try to arrange meetings between 10am - 12pm or 2pm to 4pm

Meeting Protocol

Introductions; handshakes and the exchange of business cards takes place first. Remember, the seating position is very important so always wait to be seated.

During the meeting plan and stick to a pre-defined and published agenda, If you deviate from the agenda you will create an uncomfortable atmosphere and disrupt the flow of the meeting as well as likely cause some suspicions among your Korean counterparts

Powerpoints are expected. If possible, prepare both Korean and English presentations and handouts. Many Koreans are much better at reading and understanding than they are at listening to English, providing even just English handouts or copies of your slides will help with getting your message across.

Diagrams can be useful for overcoming language barriers, especially when discussing figures.

Bring Information about your company, in Korean. A Company Introduction brochure or handout is expected and welcomed.

TIP: Follow up after the meeting with a thank you note and with any meeting points that you agreed to follow up with.

Dress code

Appearance is very important, and Koreans tend to dress quite formally. Business dress is quite conservative although among the startup community it is more relaxed.

Men usually wear dark-coloured business suits, ties and white shirts. Jewellery for men should be kept to a minimum – a watch and a wedding ring is fine. Women should also dress conservatively and in subdued colours.

These days, especially in the startup ecosystem, people are less formal and it is refreshing to see older Korean startup CEOs in running shoes and jeans, although most will still wear a semi-casual suit jacket.

TIP: Dress conservatively for your first meeting.

Bowing and handshakes

Koreans bow to those senior to them as a greeting and as a sign of respect.

The junior person initiates the bow.

The bow that is returned from the more senior person, is usually less deep. That being said, when meeting for the first time, and increasingly common these days, Koreans will shake hands.

In order to show respect, individuals support their right forearms with their left hand when offering to shake hands.

Greet the person with the highest status first, followed by the oldest when meeting a group of Koreans.

Correct form

To Bow, bend from the waist to an angle of between 30 and 45 degrees from vertical and hold the pose for a few seconds. Your hands should be placed on the side of your torso and legs.

TIP: To make identifying who to greet first easier, note that the individual with the highest status usually enters a room first.

Business cards

The exchange of business cards remain an essential part of initial meetings as it allows Koreans to quickly determine their counterpart's all-important position, title and position in the all-important hierarchy.

Exchanging business cards takes place with the initial greeting, while still standing. The rules are simple; politely hand a business card over with two hands, and receive one in return.

But it doesn't stop there. After receiving the card don't just put it into a pocket or your wallet; take a few seconds to review names and titles.

If you are sitting down, place it on the table in front of you for the duration of the meeting.

If you are standing, hold it carefully in your hand. Never give a business card back after receiving it, and never write on it, treat it as something of value to avoid upsetting your Korean counterparts.

TIP: Before a Korean Business Trip, try getting one side of your Business cards printed in Korean. Your hosts will be impressed.

Gift giving

In Korea, the importance of a relationship can be expressed through gift-giving, which is always welcomed.

Gifts should always be properly wrapped and presented with two hands. This is really important.

Don't be surprised if your gift is not opened immediately, it is considered polite to place a gift on the table and open it later, sometimes after the guests have left. Between close friends, gifts are opened excitedly as you would expect.

The importance of colour

Traditionally, the royal colours, red or yellow, were used for wrapping gifts, so Koreans will appreciate this choice of colour or you can use colours that represent happiness: yellow or pink. Avoid green, white or black wrapping paper.

Avoid Red Ink

Never sign a card in red ink.

Red ink is reserved for writing the names of the deceased.

Therefore, one should never write a person's name in red ink, especially the name of a person you are trying to do business with!

Building relationships

Building relationships is essential for doing business in Korea.

Developing relationships is usually done through informal social gatherings that generally involve a lot of eating and drinking.

Although these gatherings may seem informal they are also used as an opportunity to discuss business in a more relaxed and friendly way, so polite, respectful behaviour is required and expected.

Koreans feel a closer bond after they have eaten a meal and drank alcohol together. If you don't drink, try to participate in one toast during the meal.

If you cannot drink alcohol at all, your Korean hosts will understand so don't feel under too much pressure.

These days many Koreans don't drink, especially for religious reasons. Just be honest and say why you don't drink.

Simply, 'not liking' alcohol is not really considered a good enough reason. Health or religious reasons are.

TIP: You can ask for cider (sprite) in your shot glass so that you can at least join in with the multiple toasts during the course of the meal.

Dinner Invitations

Always accept dinner invitations as Koreans will have put a lot of thought into the venue and how they want to use the opportunity to conduct business with you.

Business entertainment tends to be reserved for the people directly involved, so it is not common to extend the invitation to spouses.

The host will usually order the food, and when it arrives wait until the host invites you to start.

At the end of the meal, the host will pay.

The other party can offer to pay for the second round, coffee or more alcohol, or a meal at a future date.

TIP: Sometimes an acquaintance will suggest you have coffee, a meal, or a drink together 'soon'. But they may just be being polite. If you want to get together, invite them back. But remember the 'guest' is treated by the person giving the invitation.

The Dark Side of Business

There is a dark side to tax-deductible business 'entertainment' in Korea, although it is becoming less common in business negotiations and after-work entertainment.

However, there are still plenty of establishments offering a range of services for businessmen, from karaoke clubs where young pretty girls serve you drinks, to business rooms or salons where girls will entertain and perform additional services.

Of course, there are seemingly endless opportunities for hedonism in brothels and massage parlours and through escort services, which although illegal are blatantly advertised everywhere across the length and breadth of the country. Many will refuse entry to foreigners.

If you are invited to Karaoke by a business associate it will most likely be an innocent experience of poor singing and overpriced side dishes, but one should be aware that seedier establishments and practices are also commonplace.

Koreans tend to be less open about this style of entertainment with foreigners.

Only once in my time in Korea did I find myself invited to a bar where the menu included additional human options with horrendously overpriced whisky, squid and peanuts.

Home Invitations

If you're invited to a Korean's home then it is a great honour and should be accepted as such.

You should take gifts such as fruit, good quality chocolates or flowers and as always present the gift with two hands.

Gifts are not opened immediately when received and will be done so later, so don't assume your gift is unwelcome if it is swiftly placed to the side.

TIP: Always offer a gift with two hands.

Dining Etiquette

On the whole, dining etiquette in Korea is similar to that of most countries. Don't blow your nose at the table, don't chew with your mouth open and so on. Although don't be surprised if your Korean host noisily slurps on their cold noodles, it just means they are enjoying them.

Utensils
Chopsticks and spoons are used for eating. You will rarely see a knife on the table in Korea. You may see scissors and tongs.
One Rule to be observed for the visiting foreigner is never leave chopsticks sticking into your rice bowl. This represents offering food to deceased relatives, so is therefore both shocking and uncomfortable for people to see.
When not using chopsticks to eat, place them on the chopstick rests or to the side of your place setting when you are not using them.

Serving
Don't serve yourself at the start of the meal or start eating before the host initiates it.

Always put food onto your plate or bowl, from a serving dish, before eating it.

Avoid picking up food with your fingers.

Use only the right hand when passing food around the table.

Mobile Phones
Koreans also tend to use their mobile phones during meetings and dinner more frequently than you would expect in the west.

Paying the bill

When it comes to settling the bill, the host will usually pay for the meal. Nevertheless, a good-natured argument over who will pay is to be expected.

It is also polite for the foreigner to offer a reciprocal dinner invitation.

TIP: Avoid discussing business during a meal, or at least wait until the host raises the subject.

Uniquely Korean traits

Korean society, as I have mentioned, is based on Confucian values and the Korean language has many single concept untranslatable words to describe these values.

There are many factors that affect relationships in Korea and these also exist within company structures.

Koreans observe deep respect for those in senior positions, who will most likely be older, those who attended the same university (seniors), and those who joined the company before them.

I have heard some Koreans say that some of the following concepts are unique to Koreans while others admit that many non-Koreans just care less about them.

Korea is a collective society so Koreans are sensitive to how actions affect others, whereas in the west we tend to be more individualistic.

TIP: Be mindful and respectful of Korean culture, and try to have an open mind in accepting that things may not be the same as at home.

Maintaining face

For Koreans, maintaining face is important to business and social relationships. Criticising or patronising someone in front of their peers is considered very offensive. As is losing one's temper.

If you want to succeed in Business, avoid doing these at all costs.

Gibun (기분)

Gibun describes one's feelings or one's current emotional state or temperament and is closely associated with personal pride. One's gibun can be hurt by others actions.

Nunchi (눈치)

Nunchi, is a joining of the words "eye" and "measure" and is an important concept in Korean culture. It is basically the awareness of the feelings of those around you. Nunchi and gibun are closely related.

Nunchi is something you have or do not have.

If Koreans appraise you as having nunchi you will be respected for it.

Nunchi is basically knowing when people think you are an ass.

Jeong (정)

Jeong is a combination of deep affection, concern, understanding, loyalty, warmth, or an emotional connection to someone or something.

You can feel jeong for your family, friends, lovers, teachers, coworkers, strangers and even for places and objects.

If nunchi is knowing when people think you are an ass, Jeong is not being an ass.

Han (한)

Han is a combination of sorrow, anger, and helplessness caused by the forces of oppression and the hope of overcoming them.

Han is experienced by the marginalized, the bullied high-school student and the worker with an unfair boss.

Therefore, han is a reaction to others' lack of nunchi and jeong.

TIP: Koreans enjoy talking about these concepts and demonstrating that you are interested and have an understanding of them will lead to interesting conversations and respect from your Korean acquaintances. But accept that you will never understand them as well as they do.

Getting a Job in Korea

I see this question come up on Facebook groups for foreigners in Korea, all the time. "How can I get a job in Korea?" "How do I get a non-teaching Job in Korea?", " I don't speak Korean, can I get a job in Korea?", "Are there any Korean companies that will employ non-Koreans in X role"?

All these questions are both the same in every country and also unique to Korea. - I realise how stupid that sounds but let me explain.

Getting a job, any job anywhere in the world requires you to do 2 things.

1. Connect with companies that have opportunities
2. Be able to demonstrate that you can provide value.

Let's look at number 1, You need to find out which companies are looking to employ people, Job bulletin boards, LinkedIn, Headhunters, Business communities, etc.

And for number two, well that is down to you - do you have the skills, and experience that someone else needs?

Korean Resume Layout

이력서

			지원분야	JOB POSITION/GRADE	
PHOTO	이름(한글)	KOREAN NAME	이름(영문)	ENGLISH NAME	
	주민등록번호	NATIONAL ID NUMBER	성별	GENDER	
	주소	ADDRESS			
	생년월일	YYYY 년 MM 월 DD 일	전화번호	PHONE NUMBER	
	이메일	EMAIL@ADDRESS.com	핸드폰	MOBILE NUMBER	

학력사항

재학기간	출신학교	학력	학과	졸업구분	소재지
EDUCATION PERIOD	SCHOOL NAME	EDUCATION	SUBJECT	LEVEL	LOCATION
START ~ END	SCHOOL NAME	EDUCATION	SUBJECT	LEVEL	LOCATION
2010.3 ~ 2013.2	SCHOOL NAME	EDUCATION	SUBJECT	LEVEL	LOCATION

경력사항

근무기간	회사명	직위	담당업무	퇴직사유
EMPLOYMENT PERIOD	COMPANY NAME	JOB GRADE	RESPONSIBILITIES	REASON FOR LEAVING
START ~ END	COMPANY NAME	JOB GRADE	RESPONSIBILITIES	REASON FOR LEAVING
2013.6 ~ 2018.10	COMPANY NAME	JOB GRADE	RESPONSIBILITIES	REASON FOR LEAVING

기타사항

			자격면허	취득일자	인증기관
종교	RELIGION		CERTIFICATIONS	2010.3 ~ 2013.2	LOCATION
취미	HOBBIES		CERTIFICATIONS	2008년 8월	LOCATION
특기	SPECIALITY			년 월	
결혼	MARITAL STATUS			년 월	
보훈대상	MILITARY AWARD				

병역

병역구분	MILITARY SERVICE CLASSIFICATION	군별	PROVINCE	신체	HEIGHT cm	최종	WEIGHT KG
사유	REASON	범과	CLASS		시력 좌 LEFT	혈액형	BLOOD TYPE 형
복무기간	PERIOD OF SERVICE YYYY.M ~ YYYY.M	계급			VISION 우 RIGHT	색맹	COLOR BLIND? X/O

가족사항

관계	성명	연령	최종학력	직업	근무처	동거여부
배우자	SPOUSE NAME	AGE	EMPL. GRADE	ROLE/INDUSTRY	POSITION	LIVING TOGETHER?
자	ELDEST SON	AGE	SCHOOL GRADE	JOB / STUDENT		O/X
녀	DAUGHTER	11	SCHOOL GRADE	JOB / STUDENT		O/X

상기 내용은 사실임을 확인합니다.

2019년 10월 일

작성자: 박지고 (인)

As you can see the format of a Korean Resume is quite different. And includes some details that would even be illegal in some countries. Height, Weight, Spouse's Job, Religion, and (although becoming less common) a photo of the applicant. You will often find that a company have their own format of Resume/CV and, sometimes extensive, questionnaire, or application pack.

However, this is a popular layout for a Korean resume (이력서). If you are in Korea you can buy a printed form, with an envelope for creating your CV at Daiso (a popular inexpensive general goods store).

You will also most likely be asked to submit a '자기소개서' personal introduction statement. In some cases (especially for graduate roles) an application essay is also requested, this can often be many pages long and is probably never read and maybe even judged by its weight rather than merit.

Headhunters

Headhunters are a big thing in Korea. In the UK a headhunter is usually only concerned with High profile executive jobs. They pursue executive talent and match them with organisations looking to recruit. In Korea the term headhunter is a bit of a 'Konglish' expression. A headhunter is simply a recruiter. But due to the social traits of Korean society, it is the relationship that the 'headhunter' has with the company that gets you in the door. However, 2/3 of the Jobs I got in Korea, were without the help of a Headhunter. I was equally successful in applying through a Job board and in Networking, the latter probably more successful. To be honest, I didn't have *that* many different Jobs in Korea, but I explored a lot of opportunities and in launching my own business I can testify that networking is probably THE most effective strategy.

As I also point out elsewhere in this book, in business an introduction by a mutual acquaintance is the best way to establish a business relationship in Korea. This is why Headhunters are so popular, and necessary.

Recruiters and Job finding resources

You can find a Job in Korea in many different ways. Like elsewhere in the world, personal introductions and headhunters help, but it is possible to find a job using Job boards, The following are Korean sites, but most of the ones listed are accessible to English speakers at least, in part. LinkedIn is also becoming a popular site to find open roles.

Top Job Sites

Job Korea
Korean: 잡코리아
https://www.jobkorea.co.kr/

Saramin
Korean: 사람인
https://www.saramin.co.kr/

Incruit
Korean: 인크루트
https://www.incruit.com/

Career
Korean: 커리어
http://www.career.co.kr/

Alba cheonguk
Korean: 알바천국
http://www.alba.co.kr/

Worknet
Korean: 워크넷
https://www.work.go.kr/seekWantedMain.do

Workplus
Korean: 교용복지플러스세터
https://www.workplus.go.kr/index.do

Albamon
Korean: 알바몬
https://www.albamon.com/

Dave's ESL Cafe
https://www.eslcafe.com/

PeoplenJob
Korean: 피플앤잡 (외국기업 취업전문 사이트)
https://www.peoplenjob.com/

Worknplay
https://www.theworknplay.com/

English Language Teaching Recruiters

While this book is about doing business in Korea, it is important to note that English Language Teaching is a huge industry. And while for many it is a gap year destination, there are a lot of people who have made a business (and successful life) out of Teaching English in Korea. And I suspect, with the growth of Ed-Tech, that this will be a growth industry in years to come. Or maybe you do want to teach English in Korea, this section is for you.

List of ESL Recruiters

Korvia Consulting
http://korvia.com/

Gone2Korea
http://www.gone2korea.com/

Adventure Teaching
http://www.adventureteaching.com/

Footprints Recruiting
http://www.footprintsrecruiting.com/

Government Teaching programs

EPIK
English Program in Korea
http://www.epik.go.kr/

The Korean Startup Ecosystem

It is not by chance that Korea has the best startup ecosystem in Asia. In 2015, the Korean government established plans to position South Korea as a regional start-up hub by placing $3bn USD on the table. In 2017 it pledged to establish a $9bn USD venture fund made up of public and private finances. And in subsequent years, on average, has contributed $2bn USD. This bold commitment to the start-up community has firmly positioned South Korea as having the highest government backing per capita for startups. There is an impressive list of government agencies (below) tasked with supporting startups. There are a number of corporate funds with several routes to funding, free office space, free legal and financial advice, and acceleration programs specifically aimed at foreign companies

In recent years Google, SparkLabs, Facebook (Meta), and other big names have also set up operations in Seoul. All this has fostered a fantastic list of over 20 companies that have made it to unicorn status. This has placed Korea 10th in the world unicorn league table.

What makes Korea so great for startups?

Economy

Top 15 Global Economy (GDP over US$1 TN) 2 BILLION CONSUMERS WITHIN A 3-HOUR FLIGHT

Despite its relatively short history as an economic powerhouse Korea ranks in the top 15 global economies. Speak to a Korean over the age of 40 for any length about the economy they will probably talk about 3 things; the Korean war, hard work, and being a shrimp between two whales. The Korean war came after centuries of isolation and oppression placing Korea behind Western ideals of development. The devastation of the Korean war left Korea as one of the world's poorest nations. As you walk around the centre of Seoul today, 65 years after an armistice ended fighting on the peninsula today's Korea couldn't be more different. Home to flagship designer boutique stores, internationally renowned modern architecture is much like any other major city, but with a pleasing and uniquely Korean flavour. Its days as the shrimp between production behemoths China and Japan are definitely numbered if not firmly resigned to history. Its location serves as a hub for the Asia region with more than 2 billion financially solvent and hungry consumers.

Infrastructure

Due to its excellent infrastructure, reasonable cost of living and proximity to Japan and China South Korea is considered one of the most comfortable places in Asia. It is no secret that Korea has the fastest average internet speed in the world. Akamai Technologies 'State of the Internet' report revealed that in 2017 Korea's average speed of 28.6 Mbit/s was a massive four times the world average. But that's not all, perhaps more of an achievement is 99.5% of Korean households have internet access and according to data published by OECD, over 40 Million mobile Internet users, who from March 2019 had access to 5G connectivity.

The rest of Korea's infrastructure is not left behind with the total length of national highways in South Korea reaching approximately 14 million kilometres in 2017 and there is also an extensive and affordable rail network connecting Korea's main cities, ports, airports and tourist sites. South Korea is the third country in the world to operate a commercial maglev train providing high-speed connections to major cities.

Population

There are 53 M People in Korea and 26M live in the greater Seoul area. A bustling metropolis of tech-obsessed highly educated citizens, each with a smartphone and credit card. Koreans are early adopters, quick to propel trends about new products through word-of-mouth an active influential community of netizens.

Korea has the world's most tech-obsessed highly educated population boasting 65% of the nation with college degrees and with high numbers of those with International Education they are Sophisticated, Demanding Tech Consumers. With reasonable Levels Of English, especially among startups and the young. Korea is becoming popular across Asia and beyond with its highly exportable culture of high fashion, and beauty.

Global Business player

Korea enjoys FTAs (Free Trade Agreements) with 52 Countries and is home to an increasing number of popular and desirable cosmetics brands and numerous global leaders such as;

Samsung, the world's largest exporter of semi-conductor chips and Apple's leading supplier. Samsung also dominates as the largest smartphone manufacturer, based on recent figures with 23.3% market share.

Posco, is the world's fourth largest steel exporter handling 7% and over 40 Million Tonnes of crude steel.

Hyundai is the world's 5th largest Automaker, based on annual sales when you include its subsidiary, KIA.

LG, combined with Samsung make South Korea the top exporter of LCD screens with 40% of the market share.

Korea can also lay claim to producing 6% of the world's total production of electrical goods, 29% of the world's, shipbuilding exports and as home to one of the world's busiest ports, is an important player in the global supply chain.

Korean startups going global

The obvious aim of many Korean start-ups is to 'Go Global' or become 'unicorns' in recent years there has been an explosion of Korean companies that have made it to be internationally recognised names and an impressive stable of unicorns. To qualify as a Unicorn, a startup must have a valuation of over $1 Billion USD and be privately owned.

Korea is now 9th in the world with 22 Unicorns.*

Korean Unicorns

- ☐ Yanolja (Travel/Hotel) — Value: **$9 bn**
- ☐ Dunamu (Crypto Exchange-Upbit)(Fin-Tech) — Value: **$8.5 bn**
- ☐ Viva Republica (Toss) (Fin-Tech) — Value: **$6.9 bn**
- ☐ Yello Mobile (Marketing/Data Solutions) — Value: **$4 bn**
- ☐ Karrot Market (hyperlocal commerce) — Value: **$2.7 bn**
- ☐ Market Kurly (Fresh food) — Value: **$2.4 bn**
- ☐ WeMakePrice (eCommerce) — Value: **$2.33 bn**
- ☐ Musinsa (Online Fashion) — Value: **$2.2 bn**
- ☐ L&P Cosmetic (Cosmetics) — Value: **$1.78 bn**
- ☐ SendBird — Value: **$1.78 bn**
- ☐ GPClub (Cosmetics) — Value: **$1.32 bn**
- ☐ SOCAR — Value: **$1.1 bn**
- ☐ Zigbang (Property-Tech) — Value: **$1 bn**
- ☐ TMON (eCommerce) — Value: **$1 bn**
- ☐ SmartStudy (Ed-Tech) — Value: **$1 bn**

*I edited this list several times while writing this book, but I have tried to keep it as upto date as possible

Launching a startup in Korea

If you are thinking about launching a startup in Korea, you are in luck. Because Korea wants you. There are numerous startup Hubs in Korea. These used to be restricted to Seoul but now Busan and Jeju are establishing themselves as government-backed startup hubs. Jeju is an interesting location, a southern island resort with a sub-tropical climate, and an interesting visa exemption policy, making it an ideal base for international startups and digital nomads. You may have to wait a few more years for it to become established, but certainly, one to watch. On the mainland, Busan is also a very attractive proposition. This coastal town is the 2nd largest in Korea, has excellent transport links and has its own international air and sea ports. Busan also is one of the words busiest shipping ports.

Exactly how to launch a startup in Korea will vary a lot depending on; the type of business, your level of investment, and your personal circumstances - such as nationality and visa status. So I am not intending to write a guide on how to launch a startup in Korea, and besides, there are many people who are better qualified to tell you how to go about that.

But hopefully, the following insights and resources will help you start that journey.

Korean Global Startups network and investment

According to The Ministry of SMEs and Startups, the Korean government invests, on average, $2bn a year in startups, with a reported $3.6bn invested in 2019. (Source: Ministry of SMEs and Startups)

The Ministry of SMEs and Startups' mission is to develop and implement government policies over the following three areas:
- Promoting Business Growth
- Fostering Business Start-ups
- Supporting Micro Enterprises

You can find up-to-date information on investment and government policy here: https://www.mss.go.kr/site/eng/main.do

Some other places to look are:*
Gov / Official:
- https://www.investkorea.org
- https://www.born2global.com/
- https://www.kotra.or.kr/english/index.do
- https://www.kised.or.kr/_eng/

Community:
- https://www.seoulstartups.com/
- https://impactcollective.earth

Media:
- https://www.seoulz.com/

*Not an exhaustive list, but ones that I know, like, and trust

Korean Government led Startup programs for foreigners

OASIS
Overall Assistance for Start-up Immigration System
http://www.oasisvisa.com/

K-Startup Grand Challenge
https://www.k-startupgc.org/

TIPS
Tech Incubator Program for Startup
http://www.jointips.or.kr/global/

Born2global Startup Program
https://www.born2global.com/

Seoul Global Center
Incubation and Big Think Demo Day. Contact for general advice or support.
https://global.seoul.go.kr/web/main.do

Registering a Business in Korea

You will be pleased to know, registering a business in Korea is inexpensive and relatively easy. There are 2 types of business recognised in Korea, Individual and Corporation.

In Korean, an individual business is called 개인사업자 (gaein sa ob ja) and a corporation is called a 법인사업자 (Bobin sa ob ja).

An individual business is what you may know as a sole proprietor, and a corporation can also be a single-person owner business.

From a Korean perspective, a Corporation is considered more trustworthy and will be taken more seriously than an individual business.

While still relatively cheap setting up a corporation is slightly more complex and expensive than an individual business.

The main differences between the two types of business are related to Tax declaration and payment and personal use of profit that your business generates.

With a Private or individual business, all income (profit) is yours and tax is declared half-yearly.

For a Corporation, you will need to employ an accounting system and record and declare all expenses. But you will not be able to personally use any of the money generated. You will need to issue share dividends.

Importantly you will only pay 10% tax on earnings under 200 Million won.

To obtain a business licence for either type of business it is necessary to first register with the district office, then with the tax office.

There are a number of government organisations and systems in place to help set up a business in Korea these range from visa support, bank loans, to startup funding.

As these policies and support systems change often, I have not included details in this book.

It is, therefore, best to check with the relevant agency websites for the latest information. Below is a list of websites where you can look for information about support for starting a business in Korea.

www.seoulshinbo.co.kr

www.semas.or.kr

www.sbiz.or.kr

www.global.seoul.go.kr

TIP: Register your business as a corporation, it will cost a little more, but you will pay less tax and people will take you and your business more seriously.

Marketing in Korea

Not Surprisingly marketing in Korea also has its specific quirks. Korea has its own search engine, blogging and advertising platform, in some ways similar to google, but at the same time very unique.

Naver is the go-to place for information in Korea and like google this has also become a verb, "Naver it" is the war cry of curious Korean keyboard warriors.

Naver is extremely powerful in Korea and provides all the expected services such as Blogging, Map, and search.

If you are launching a business in Korea then it is essential that your business can be found through a simple Naver search.

SEO exists in Naver but as "Paid Results" take the top spot, success in Korea takes some investment, a business registration number, and a loyal following.

Yes, Reviews and testimonials are of utmost importance in Korea, and to succeed you need to get people talking about your business… on Naver.

Naver does display organic search results, which appear after the paid listings, but often these won't be shown until page three or four of the search results.

Naver's CPC (Cost Per Click) platform is called Power Link and is a paid advertising system that operates with a public bidding style.

Fees vary by keyword popularity and the keywords cannot be capped individually, although the total can be capped to allow for budgeting. You will need to pay in advance for power link campaigns.

Naver shows the top 10 results for a given keyword on page 1 on PC and the Top 3 results on Mobile.

Bear this in mind when planning campaigns and budgets as Korea is heavily mobile-first.

Naver has a number of categories that could display keyword results, Naver Cafe, Naver Blogs, Naver Encyclopedia, Naver maps, and Naver Images, but remember that Naver Organic results are shown way below any paid listing, on any category.

Another, probably obvious, point I should make clear is that Naver searches and results are in the Korean Language. So you will likely need some local assistance to get your Korean marketing machine up and running.

TIP: Register for a NAVER email account and you can access all their platforms including a power link account.

Index

Introduction — 3

    Who is this book for? — 3

    Why did I write this book? — 4

    About me — 5

Note to the reader — 5

South Korea — 6

Korean Language and Useful Phrases — 7

    Vowels — 8

    Consonants — 8

    Diphthongs — 10

    Greetings and Goodbyes — 11

    Introductions — 12

    Polite words — 13

    Learning More — 13

    Days — **14**

    Days of the week — **14**

Numbers — 15

    Counting — 16

    Sino-Korean numbers — 16

Native Korean Numbers	**18**
Counting words	19
Respect, Age, and status	**21**
Positions and Titles	**23**
Working Hours	**25**
The rules	25
The reality	25
Night work	26
Hweshik (Staff Meal)	**27**
Gender Equality	**29**
Korean names	**30**
Introductions	**31**
Meetings	**33**
Meeting Protocol	34
Dress code	**35**
Bowing and handshakes	**36**
Correct form	36
Business cards	**37**
Gift giving	**39**
The importance of colour	**39**

Avoid Red Ink	39
Building relationships	40
Dinner Invitations	41
The Dark Side of Business	42
Home Invitations	43
Dining Etiquette	44
Utensiles	44
Serving	44
Mobile Phones	44
Paying the bill	45
Uniquely Korean traits	46
Maintaining face	47
Gibun (기분)	47
Nunchi (눈치)	47
Jeong (정)	48
Han (한)	48
Getting a Job in Korea	49
Korean Resume Layout	50
Headhunters	52
Recruiters and Job finding resources	53

Top Job Sites	53
Job Korea	53
Saramin	53
Incruit	53
Career	53
Alba cheonguk	53
Worknet	54
Workplus	54
Albamon	54
Dave's ESL Cafe	54
PeoplenJob	54
Worknplay	54
English Language Teaching Recruiters	55
List of ESL Recruiters	55
Korvia Consulting	55
Gone2Korea	55
Adventure Teaching	55
Footprints Recruiting	55
Government Teaching programs	55
EPIK	55

The Korean Startup Ecosystem	**56**
What makes korea so great for startups?	57
Economy	57
Infrastructure	58
Population	59
Global Business player	60
Korean startups going global	61
Korean Unicorns (Top 15)	61
Launching a startup in Korea	62
Korean Global Startups network and investment	63
Gov / Official:	63
Community:	63
Korean Government led Startup programs for foreigners	64
OASIS	64
K-Startup Grand Challenge	64
TIPS	64
Born2global Startup Program	64
Seoul Global Center	64
Registering a Business in Korea	**65**
Marketing in Korea	**67**
Index	**69**

www.ingramcontent.com/pod-product-compliance
Lightning Source LLC
Chambersburg PA
CBHW050256220526
45465CB00002B/702